Inbox Influence

A Practical Guide to Mastering Email Marketing

How to Build, Grow, and Monetize an Email List for Long-Term Business Success

by

Debbie Blower

Published by

Debbie Blower Publishing

Canada

debbieblowerpublishing@gmail.com

"Because while trends come and go, email influence lasts."

Contents

Published by:

Debbie Blower Publishing

Canada

ISBN: 978-0-9739637-4-8

Printed in Canada.

This publication is intended to provide general information and practical guidance on email marketing. It is not intended as a substitute for professional business, financial, or legal advice. The author and publisher disclaim any liability arising directly or indirectly from the use of the information contained within this book.

For all the entrepreneurs building their dream, one email at a time.

Disclaimer

The information in this book is provided for educational and informational purposes only. It is not intended as, and should not be considered a substitute for, professional advice, whether business, financial, marketing, or legal.

While every effort has been made to ensure the accuracy and completeness of the content at the time of publication, the author and publisher make no representations or warranties of any kind and accept no liability for any errors or omissions. Readers are encouraged to consult with qualified professionals before making business, financial, or legal decisions.

The strategies, examples, and resources shared in this book are based on personal experience, industry practices, and available data. Results may vary depending on individual effort, market conditions, and other factors beyond the author's control. Success in business and marketing is never guaranteed.

Mention of specific companies, platforms, or tools does not constitute an endorsement. All trademarks and registered trademarks are the property of their respective owners.

Dedication

To every entrepreneur who's ever stayed up late chasing an idea,

to the dreamers who keep showing up even when it feels impossible,

and to the small business owners building something real —

one email, one connection, one brave step at a time.

This book is for you.

— Debbie

Acknowledgments

Writing this book has been a journey — and like all journeys, I didn't take it alone.

To my family, thank you for your patience, encouragement, and constant belief in me. Your support has been the foundation that allowed me to pour myself into these pages.

To my friends and fellow entrepreneurs who cheered me on (and reminded me to keep going when I doubted myself), I'm deeply grateful. You kept me accountable and inspired me with your own stories of resilience and creativity.

To my readers — whether this is your first step into email marketing or your hundredth — thank you for trusting me to guide you. This book exists because of you and for you.

And finally, to every late-night cup of coffee that fueled another chapter — I couldn't have done it without you either.

— Debbie

Series Preface

The Human Side of Smart Selling

The Heart Centered Direct Sales Series Direct sales is not simply about selling products. At its best, it is about people—about trust, connection, and the courage to build a business rooted in both strategy and soul.

The Heart Centered Direct Sales Series was created to reimagine what business can feel like when compassion and clarity lead the way. Each book serves as a lantern—illuminating one part of the path and offering practical tools, gentle encouragement, and creative inspiration for direct sellers at every stage of their journey.

Across twelve volumes, this series explores the many dimensions of building a thriving business with heart: from mastering email and content to embracing AI as a compassionate guide; from creating welcoming communities to nurturing loyal customers; from gentle follow-up to confident leadership; from everyday systems to the lasting legacy you leave behind.

You may choose to read these books in order or begin with the one that speaks most to your current season. Each stands alone, but together they form a larger story—a vision of direct sales done differently: with kindness at the center and courage lighting the way.

May these books remind you that you don't need to sacrifice authenticity to succeed. You can grow a business that not only prospers but also uplifts everyone it touches.

With gratitude for your journey,

Debbie Blower

📖 Introduction

Why Email Marketing Still Works

They've said it for years — "Email is dead."

But here's the truth: email marketing isn't just alive, it's thriving.

Those who understand how to use it effectively aren't just surviving in business — they're scaling, growing, and building real relationships with their audience.

You don't need a massive ad budget, a million followers, or the latest growth hack to succeed. You need a system that lets you connect directly with people who want what you offer. That system is email. And in this book, I'm going to show you how to use it to build, grow, and monetize your audience — all while keeping your strategy authentic, simple, and sustainable.

📦 Reflection Box
Think about your own inbox.
Which emails do you always open?
Which ones do you instantly delete?
What makes the difference?

Why I Wrote This Book

Like many people in business, I used to chase every shiny object. New platforms, trending content strategies, algorithms that changed overnight — I tried them all.

But no matter what I did, one thing remained constant: email always worked. It delivered sales. It built trust. And best of all, I owned the relationship.

I've written this book because I believe entrepreneurs, creators, and small business owners deserve to grow their brands without depending on platforms they don't control. Email gives you that freedom.

🏆 *Gentle Reminder*
You don't own your social media following.
You do own your email list.

Why Email Still Works (Better Than Ever)

The inbox isn't just a place for newsletters anymore. It's where trust is built, stories are told, and offers are made.

Here's why email is still your smartest marketing move:

➢ Direct access to your audience — no algorithms deciding if your message is seen.
➢ Higher ROI than nearly any other digital channel.
➢ Automation that works while you sleep.
➢ Ownership of your list — no platform can take it away.
➢ Personalization that actually resonates.

What This Book Will Help You Do

Whether you're starting from zero or already have a small list, this book is your hands-on guide to mastering the inbox.

You'll learn how to:

➤ Choose the best email marketing platform for your needs
➤ Create lead magnets that grow your list on autopilot
➤ Write emails people actually want to read
➤ Set up automated sequences that build relationships and drive sales
➤ Segment your list for smarter campaigns
➤ Avoid spam filters and stay compliant
➤ Turn subscribers into paying customers — repeatedly
➤ Measure what matters and continuously improves

✎ Quick Exercise
Grab a notebook and write down:
☞ "What's the ONE main thing I want email marketing to do for my business this year?"

Keep this answer handy — we'll revisit it later.

Who This Book Is For

This book is for you if:

➤ You want to grow a business without relying solely on social media
➤ You're tired of marketing that doesn't convert
➤ You want a predictable, scalable system for generating leads and revenue
➤ You believe in building something long-term, not just chasing quick wins

Whether you're a solopreneur, coach, content creator, or small business owner, Inbox Influence will help you take email from an afterthought to a revenue-generating machine.

🗃 *Reflection Box*
Where do you see yourself right now?
Total beginner, with no list yet?
Growing, but not consistent?
Already sending emails, but want to improve results?
Circle one — and let's start from there.

How to Use This Book

Each chapter is designed to build on the last, guiding you from foundational principles to advanced strategies.

Read it in order the first time, or skip to the parts that matter most to you now.

Use the templates, swipe files, and resources at the end to take action quickly.

Take notes. Try things. Test. Adapt.

🌱 *Gentle Reminder*
Trends come and go.
Email influence lasts.

☑ Introduction Action Step:

Write down your #1 goal for your email marketing journey. Place it somewhere visible — above your desk, on your fridge, or inside your planner.

📖 Chapter 1

Getting Started — Understanding the Basics

"Don't build your business on borrowed land."
— Every smart digital marketer, ever

Before you start designing lead magnets or crafting killer subject lines, you need to understand the why behind email marketing — and how it actually works. This chapter is your foundation. It's where we cut through the noise, define the essentials, and get you thinking strategically about what email can do for your business.

This isn't theory. This is the start of your system.

📦 Reflection Box
Right now, how do you communicate with your audience?
Social posts?
Ads?
Word of mouth?

How would things change if you could speak to them directly — without relying on an algorithm?

What Is Email Marketing, Really?

Email marketing isn't "sending a monthly newsletter" or "blasting promotions." And it's definitely not dead.

Email marketing is about building trust at scale.

At its core, it is:

➤ Permission-based communication
➤ Value-driven content delivery
➤ Automated and scalable

💡 Key Insight

Every subscriber is a person who trusted you with access to their inbox. Treat that space with care.

➤ Focused on conversion

When someone joins your list, they've said: "Yes, I want to hear from you." That kind of permission is powerful — and rare.

Why Email Still Matters in 2025

We live in the attention economy. Social media is noisy. Ads are everywhere. Algorithms shift weekly. People scroll endlessly — and forget what they saw five minutes later.

But the inbox? That's personal.

The latest data shows email delivers:

- ➤ $36–$42 ROI for every $1 spent
- ➤ 4x better engagement than social media posts
- ➤ 100% ownership — no platform can take it away

Key Email Marketing Terms

Here are the essentials you'll see throughout this book:

- ➤ Subscriber – Someone who's given you permission to email them
- ➤ Open Rate – % who opened your email
- ➤ Click-Through Rate (CTR) – % who clicked a link
- ➤ Opt-In – Action of signing up
- ➤ Lead Magnet – Freebie offered in exchange for an email
- ➤ Sequence / Autoresponder – Automated series of emails
- ➤ Segmentation – Categorizing your list by interest/behaviour
- ➤ Deliverability – Your ability to reach inboxes, not spam

✏️ *Quick Exercise*
Choose 3 of these terms that are new to you.
Write your own definition in plain words. Explaining it simply makes it stick.

The Role of Email in the Customer Journey

Think of your email list as a relationship timeline:

- ➢ Discovery – They find you (content, ad, referral).
- ➢ Sign-Up – They opt in.
- ➢ Nurture – You provide value and build trust.
- ➢ Offer – You present a product, service, or invitation.
- ➢ Loyalty – They buy again, refer, and stay engaged.
- ➢ Your job: guide them through each stage.

🎁 *Reflection Box*

Where do most of your leads "drop off"?

Do they find you but never sign up?

Do they sign up but never engage?

Do they engage but never buy?

Circle the stage you most need to fix.

Build Now, Sell Later

💡 Key Insight

Email is a long game. It compounds over time and works 24/7 once the system is in place.

Here's where many go wrong: they try to sell before they've earned trust.

If you focus on serving, educating, and providing value, sales will come — consistently.

What You Need to Get Started

You don't need a website, funnel, or 10,000 people. You just need:

- ➢ An email platform (we'll cover in Chapter 2)
- ➢ A clear niche or audience
- ➢ A basic understanding of what they value
- ➢ Willingness to write with purpose, not perfection

🌱 *Gentle Reminder*

Start where you are. Even 10 subscribers is a start — and often, your first 10 are the most valuable.

Action Steps for Chapter 1

- ➢ By the end of this chapter, you should:
- ➢ Understand the real purpose of email marketing
- ➢ Know the key terms and their meanings
- ➢ See how email fits into your customer journey
- ➢ Commit to building something long-term

✏️ *Quick Exercise*

Write one sentence that answers this question:

☞ What's the #1 reason I want to use email marketing in my business?

📖 Chapter 2

Choosing the Right Email Marketing Platform

"Don't choose the fanciest tool. Choose the tool you'll actually use."

There are dozens of email marketing platforms out there, and if you've ever Googled "best email marketing software," you know it can feel overwhelming. Should you use Mailchimp? ConvertKit? ActiveCampaign? Something built into your CRM?

This chapter will help you cut through the noise and make a smart, simple choice.

📦 *Reflection Box*

Think about the tools you already use in your business.

Do you love simplicity?

Do you enjoy tech, or does it frustrate you?

Do you prefer "set it and forget it" automation, or hands-on control?

The answers will guide your platform choice more than any review site.

The Big 3 Features That Matter

- ➢ When choosing a platform, focus on what actually impacts results:
- ➢ Deliverability – Can it reliably land your emails in the inbox (not spam)?
- ➢ Ease of Use – Does the interface make sense for you?
- ➢ Automation Power – Can it send sequences, tag users, and segment your list? Everything else is "nice to have."

Popular Platforms at a Glance

> ➢ Mailchimp – Well-known, good for beginners, but limited
>   automation.
> ➢ ConvertKit – Designed for creators, simple, strong for sequences.
> ➢ ActiveCampaign – Powerful automations, more advanced.
> ➢ MailerLite – Affordable, easy, great balance for small businesses.
> ➢ Klaviyo – Ecommerce-focused, integrates deeply with Shopify.
> ➢ HubSpot – Robust CRM + email, ideal for bigger businesses.

What About Free Plans?

Many platforms offer free tiers, but with limits (subscribers, sends, or
features). Free is fine to test the waters, but if you're serious, you'll want paid
features like automation and tagging sooner than later.

There's no wrong answer — just be honest with your priorities.

Matching Platform to Business Type

- ➤ Creators / Coaches / Bloggers → ConvertKit or MailerLite
- ➤ Ecommerce → Klaviyo or Shopify Email
- ➤ Service Providers / Consultants → ActiveCampaign or HubSpot
- ➤ Beginners → Mailchimp or MailerLite

💡 Key Insight

Don't pick a platform because a "guru" told you to. Pick it because it fits your business model and personality.

✏️ *Quick Exercise*
Make a simple chart with 3 columns:

Platform   *What I Like*   *What I Don't Like*

Test-drive 2 platforms this week. Write down what feels intuitive and what feels clunky.

☑ Action Steps for Chapter 2

➢ Narrow your platform options down to two.
➢ Sign up for free trials (most offer them).
➢ Test sending a welcome email.
➢ Choose the one you'll commit to for at least 6 months.

🌱 Gentle Reminder

It's not about the tool. It's about the trust you build with the tool.

📖 Chapter 3

Building a High-Quality Email List

"You don't need a big list. You need the right list."

A common mistake in email marketing is chasing numbers. Entrepreneurs brag about having 10,000 or 50,000 subscribers — but if those people never open, click, or buy, that list is dead weight.

A high-quality list of 500 engaged subscribers will outperform a cold list of 50,000 any day. This chapter will help you build your list the right way — with people who actually want to hear from you.

📦 *Reflection Box*
Think about your ideal customer.
What problem do they need solved right now?
What do they value most: saving time, saving money, or learning something new?
How would their life look different if they worked with you?
These answers will guide who belongs on your list.

Quality Over Quantity

Your goal isn't "any subscriber." It's the right subscriber.

Ask yourself: Would I be excited if this person bought from me? If not, don't chase them.

High-quality subscribers:

- ➢ Signed up for a clear reason
- ➢ Fit your target audience
- ➢ Open and engage with emails
- ➢ Likely to benefit from your offers
- ➢ Low-quality subscribers:
- ➢ Signed up just for a contest freebie
- ➢ Unrelated to your niche
- ➢ Never open your emails
- ➢ Unlikely to buy anything

💡 Key Insight

The easiest way to grow the wrong kind of list is to offer the wrong kind of lead magnet. (We'll fix that in Chapter 4!)

Where Do Subscribers Come From?

There are three main sources:

- ➢ Owned Channels – Website, blog, podcast, in-person events.
- ➢ Borrowed Channels – Social media, YouTube, online communities.
- ➢ Paid Channels – Ads (Facebook, Instagram, Google).

Start with one. Don't try to master them all at once.

🌱 *Gentle Reminder*
One reliable channel is better than five half-baked ones.

The Power of Opt-In

People must choose to join your list. Buying or renting email lists is not only illegal in many places — it's ineffective. Those people don't know you, trust you, or want your emails.

Instead, focus on opt-ins:

> ➢ Website sign-up forms
> ➢ Pop-ups or slide-ins
> ➢ Landing pages
> ➢ Social media links
> ➢ Your Instagram bio?
> ➢ Your website header?
> ➢ A QR code on your printed material?

Engagement Is the Real Goal

🎁 *Reflection Box*
Where can you add one new opt-in opportunity this week?

Building the list is only half the work. Keeping it warm is what matters.

Your first priority isn't to "grow fast." It's to grow engaged.

Tips for engagement:

> ➢ Send a welcome email right away
> ➢ Be consistent (weekly or biweekly is better than random)
> ➢ Ask questions to encourage replies
> ➢ Deliver small wins (quick tips, resources, tools)

✏️ *Quick Exercise*
Write down your ideal frequency:
☞ *"I will email my list every ____ (day/week/other)."*

Stick with it. Consistency builds trust.

The "Unsubscribe Test"

Don't fear unsubscribes. They help keep your list healthy.

If someone unsubscribes, it means they weren't the right fit. That's okay.

💡 Key Insight

Every unsubscribe makes room for someone who is aligned with your message.

✅ Action Steps for Chapter 3

- ➤ Define who belongs on your "ideal subscriber" list.
- ➤ Identify 1–2 opt-in sources you'll focus on.
- ➤ Decide on your consistent sending frequency.
- ➤ Remember: engagement > numbers.

🌱 Gentle Reminder

You're not just collecting emails. You're building relationships, one inbox at a time.

📖 Chapter 4

Crafting the Perfect Lead Magnet

"Your lead magnet is the handshake before the conversation."

If your email list is the foundation of your business, your lead magnet is the front door. It's how most subscribers will first interact with you — and it's what convinces them to hand over their precious email address.

A strong lead magnet doesn't just "get sign-ups." It attracts the right people and starts building trust immediately.

📦 *Reflection Box*

Think about the last time you downloaded something online.

Why did you want it?

Did you actually use it?

Did it make you trust that brand more? Or less?

What Makes a Lead Magnet "Perfect"?

A perfect lead magnet is:

- ➢ Relevant – It solves a problem your audience cares about right now.
- ➢ Quick – They can consume it in 5–10 minutes.
- ➢ Actionable – It helps them achieve a small win immediately.
- ➢ Aligned – It leads naturally to your paid offers.

If your lead magnet attracts the wrong people, your email list will too.

Popular Types of Lead Magnets

Checklists / Cheat Sheets – Quick, easy wins.

Templates / Swipe Files – Done-for-you shortcuts.

Guides / E-Books – Deeper dive on a specific problem.

Mini-Courses / Video Lessons – Higher perceived value, builds authority.

Quizzes – Interactive, fun, highly shareable.

Discounts / Free Trials – Great for ecommerce.

🌱 Gentle Reminder
The best lead magnet isn't the fanciest. It's the one your audience actually uses.

How to Brainstorm Your Lead Magnet

Ask these three questions:

> ➢ What does my audience struggle with most right now?
> ➢ What small win can I help them achieve quickly?
> ➢ How can I connect this win to my larger paid offer?

🗃 *Reflection Box*
Write down one product, service, or offer you sell.
Now ask: What's the very first step my customer needs before buying this?

That's a great lead magnet idea.

Naming Your Lead Magnet

Your title matters more than you think. "Free Guide" won't cut it. Instead, promise a clear result.

Examples:

> ➢ "10 Instagram Caption Formulas That Double Engagement"
> ➢ "The 5-Minute Meal Planner for Busy Moms"
> ➢ "The Beginner's Checklist to Stress-Free Tax Season"

✎ *Quick Exercise*
Draft 3 possible titles for your lead magnet.
Tip: Use this formula → [Number/Timeframe] + [Adjective] + [Result]

Delivery & Presentation

Once someone signs up, deliver your lead magnet immediately (via email or thank-you page).

Make sure it's:

- ➢ Visually clean and easy to read
- ➢ Mobile-friendly
- ➢ Action-focused (avoid fluff)

♀ Key Insight

Your lead magnet isn't the end goal. It's the on-ramp to your relationship.

☑ Action Steps for Chapter 4

- ➢ Choose 1 lead magnet idea that feels simple and valuable.
- ➢ Draft a strong, results-focused title.
- ➢ Create a quick, easy-to-use format (PDF, video, checklist).
- ➢ Set up delivery in your email platform.

⚘ Gentle Reminder

Don't spend months perfecting. Launch fast, test it, and improve later.

📖 Chapter 5

Writing Emails That Get Opened and Read

"An email unopened is a story untold."

Your list only works if people actually open and read what you send. This chapter is all about writing emails that not only avoid the dreaded "delete" button, but spark curiosity, deliver value, and keep subscribers coming back for more.

📦 *Reflection Box*
Think about your own inbox.
Which subject lines make you open instantly?
Which ones do you ignore?
How do you feel about the emails you actually read through?
The Anatomy of a Great Email
Subject Line – The door opener.
Preheader Text – The teaser.
Body Copy – The story or message.
Call-to-Action (CTA) – The "what's next."

💡 Key Insight

The subject line doesn't sell the product — it sells the open.

When these 4 parts work together, your email has impact.

Writing Subject Lines That Work

Tips for subject lines:

- ➢ Keep it short (4–8 words).
- ➢ Add curiosity, but avoid clickbait.
- ➢ Use numbers and specifics.
- ➢ Personalize when possible.

Examples:

- ➢ "Your 3-minute morning reset"
- ➢ "This almost cost me $500"
- ➢ "Hey [First Name], quick question"

🌱 *Gentle Reminder*
If you wouldn't open it yourself, don't send it.

Tone and Voice

Email isn't a corporate memo — it's a conversation.

Write like you'd write to a friend. Keep it natural, warm, and human.

- ➢ Use contractions (you'll, don't).
- ➢ Short sentences.
- ➢ Ask questions.
- ➢ Break up text with white space.

🗃 *Reflection Box*

Who do you admire for their writing style? A blogger, an author, or even a podcaster?

How can you adapt that conversational tone to your emails?

💡 Key Insight

People don't remember the pitch. They remember how your story made them feel.

[Cite your source here.]

Storytelling in Emails

Stories are sticky. Facts fade, but stories are remembered.

Share:

> ➢ Customer success stories
> ➢ Behind-the-scenes moments
> ➢ Lessons from mistakes
> ➢ Personal anecdotes that connect to your message

Calls-to-Action (CTAs)

Every email should have a purpose. That doesn't always mean selling — but it does mean leading your reader to a next step.

Examples of CTAs:

> ➢ Click a link to read more
> ➢ Reply to the email with an answer
> ➢ Download a resource
> ➢ Book a call
> ➢ Buy a product
> ➢ Keep it clear. One email = one primary CTA.

✎ Quick Exercise
Draft one simple CTA you could use in your next email.
☞ Example: "Hit reply and tell me your biggest struggle with [topic]."

The Power of Consistency

Your subscribers should learn to expect — and look forward to — your emails. Whether it's every week, every 2 weeks, or monthly, consistency builds reliability.

✅ Action Steps for Chapter 5

➢ Write 3 subject line drafts before sending any email.
➢ Use a conversational tone — imagine writing to one person.
➢ Add one story to your next email.
➢ End with a single, clear CTA.

📖 Chapter 6

Setting Up Automated Email Sequences

"Automation isn't about replacing you. It's about scaling you."

The beauty of email marketing is that you don't have to write every single email live and send it manually. With automation, you can set up smart, personalized sequences that welcome, nurture, and guide subscribers — even while you're asleep.

This chapter is about creating the backbone of your email marketing system: automated email sequences.

📦 *Reflection Box*
Think about your ideal customer journey.
What do you want a new subscriber to know about you?
What's the first small win you could help them achieve?
What path should they follow toward becoming a customer?
What Is an Email Sequence?

An email sequence (also called an autoresponder) is a series of emails sent automatically when triggered by an action, such as signing up for your lead magnet.

Types of sequences:

- ➤ Welcome Sequence – Introduces you and sets expectations.
- ➤ Nurture Sequence – Builds trust and provides value.
- ➤ Sales Sequence – Presents your offer.
- ➤ Onboarding Sequence – Helps new customers succeed.
- ➤ Re-Engagement Sequence – Revives inactive subscribers.

💡 Key Insight

Automation is not about blasting everyone the same message.
It's about sending the right message at the right time.

The Must-Have: Your Welcome Sequence

Your welcome sequence is the most important automation you'll create.

Why? Because first impressions matter.

A simple 3–5 email welcome flow could include:

- ➤ Thank You & Delivery – Give them the lead magnet, thank them warmly.
- ➤ Your Story – Share who you are and what you stand for.
- ➤ Value Piece – Deliver a tip, insight, or tool.
- ➤ Engagement Prompt – Ask them a question or invite a reply.
- ➤ Soft Offer – Introduce your product/service casually.

🌱 *Gentle Reminder*

Your welcome sequence is like a first coffee date. Don't propose marriage (hard sell) right away.

Automation Triggers

Common triggers that start a sequence:

- ➢ Subscribing to your list
- ➢ Downloading a lead magnet
- ➢ Clicking a link in an email
- ➢ Abandoning a shopping cart (ecommerce)
- ➢ Becoming a customer

📦 Reflection Box
Which trigger makes the most sense for your business right now?
Circle one:
Sign-up
Lead magnet download
Cart abandonment
First purchase
Tools to Make It Simple

Most email platforms (ConvertKit, ActiveCampaign, MailerLite, etc.) have drag-and-drop automation builders. Start simple — don't get lost in "if/then" rabbit holes until you've mastered the basics.

🖊 Quick Exercise
Sketch a simple 3-email welcome sequence on paper.
☞ Email 1: Delivery + thanks
☞ Email 2: Story + value
☞ Email 3: Invitation to connect or explore

✅ Action Steps for Chapter 6

Choose one sequence to build first (welcome is best).

> ➢ Write 3–5 short emails for it.
> ➢ Set up the trigger in your email platform.
> ➢ Test it with your own email before launching.

💡 Key Insight

Automations are assets. You create them once, and they keep working for you — forever.

📖 Chapter 7

Advanced Segmentation and Personalization

"Speak to everyone, and you'll connect with no one."

Segmentation and personalization are where email marketing goes from "mass messaging" to "meaningful conversations." Instead of treating your list as one big blob, you start talking to individuals — at scale. This is the difference between being ignored and being remembered.

📦 Reflection Box

Think about the last email you opened that felt like it was written just for you.

What made it feel personal?

Did it use your name?

Did it reference your past behaviour?

Did it feel like the sender understood you?

What Is Segmentation?

Segmentation is dividing your email list into smaller groups based on shared traits or behaviours.

Examples:

- ➤ New subscribers vs. long-term subscribers
- ➤ Customers vs. prospects
- ➤ People interested in Product A vs. Product B
- ➤ Engaged readers vs. inactive readers
- ➤ This ensures the right people get the right messages.

♀ Key Insight

Relevance is the new currency. The more relevant your emails,
the higher your engagement and conversions.

What Is Personalization?

Personalization goes beyond "Hi [First Name]." It's about tailoring the content itself to reflect the subscriber's journey, interests, or actions.

Examples:

- ➤ Recommending products based on past purchases
- ➤ Sending tips related to what they clicked
- ➤ Customizing frequency (daily tips vs. weekly digest)

🌱 *Gentle Reminder*
Personalization should feel natural, not creepy. Respect your subscriber's privacy.

Easy Ways to Segment Your List

You don't need complex data science to start. Here are beginner-friendly options:

- ➤ Tag subscribers by lead magnet they opted into
- ➤ Separate customers from non-customers
- ➤ Track clicks and segment by interest
- ➤ Identify inactive subscribers for re-engagement campaigns

---

🗐 *Reflection Box*

Which of these could you implement this month?

Lead magnet tags

Customer vs. prospect split

Click-based interest groups

Inactive subscriber clean-up

Personalization Techniques That Work

Dynamic Content – Show different sections to different groups.

Behavioural Triggers – Send emails based on clicks, purchases, or inactivity.

Tailored Offers – Recommend products/services that match interests.

✐ *Quick Exercise*

Write down one product or service you sell.

☞ Now brainstorm 2 different ways you could frame that offer for:

A new subscriber

A repeat customer

Why This Matters

Segmentation and personalization don't just improve open and click rates. They build trust. People feel seen, heard, and understood. That's what transforms a subscriber into a loyal customer.

♀ Key Insight

When subscribers feel like you "get" them, they stop seeing you as a marketer — and start seeing you as a partner.

☑ Action Steps for Chapter 7

➤ Pick one segmentation method to implement (start simple).
➤ Add a tag or field in your email platform to track it.
➤ Personalize at least one email this week (beyond just using a name).
➤ Track results and adjust.

🌱 Gentle Reminder
You don't need to personalize everything. Sometimes the most personal thing you can do is simply write with empathy.

📖 Chapter 8

A/B Testing and Analytics for Growth

"What gets measured gets improved."

The best marketers don't just guess. They test.

A/B testing (also called split testing) and email analytics are how you learn what works, what doesn't, and how to continuously grow your results.

This chapter will help you think like a scientist in your marketing — curious, experimental, and data-driven.

📦 Reflection Box
Be honest: when was the last time you actually checked your open or click-through rates?
Do you know your averages?
Do you know what "good" looks like in your niche?
Or do you just hit send and hope?
What Is A/B Testing?
A/B testing means sending two versions of an email to see which performs better.

You change one thing and measure results.

Examples:

- ➤ Subject line A vs. Subject line B
- ➤ Button text "Buy Now" vs. "Get Started"
- ➤ Image vs. no image
- ➤ Long story vs. short tip

💡 Key Insight

Never test everything at once. Change one variable at a time so you know what made the difference.

What Metrics Actually Matter?

There's a flood of numbers in your dashboard, but focus on these:

- ➤ Open Rate – Are your subject lines working?
- ➤ Click-Through Rate (CTR) – Is your content compelling?
- ➤ Conversion Rate – Are subscribers taking the action you want (buying, booking, etc.)?
- ➤ Unsubscribes – Are you losing people faster than you're gaining them?

🏺 *Gentle Reminder*
A low open rate isn't failure — it's feedback.

Benchmarks (But Don't Obsess)

Industry averages vary, but here's a rough guide:

- ➢ Open rates: 20–30% is solid
- ➢ CTR: 2–5% is healthy
- ➢ Unsubscribes: <0.5% per send is normal
- ➢ Use these as ballparks, not report cards.

🎁 *Reflection Box*

Which metric feels like your biggest weakness right now?

Open rates?

Clicks?

Conversions?

Retention?

That's the one to focus your testing on.

How to Run a Simple A/B Test

- ➢ Pick one variable (e.g., subject line).
- ➢ Write two versions.
- ➢ Split your list (most platforms do this automatically).
- ➢ Send both at the same time.
- ➢ Track results after 24–48 hours.
- ➢ Use the winner going forward.

Imagine:

- ➤ Boosting open rates by just 2% each month
- ➤ Increasing CTR by 1% per test
- ➤ Reducing unsubscribes by fine-tuning tone
- ➤ Over a year, those small wins multiply into big growth.

☑ Action Steps for Chapter 8

> Identify your weakest metric.
> Run one simple A/B test this week.
> Record results in a tracker.
> Apply the winner to future campaigns.

🍸 *Gentle Reminder*

Done is better than perfect. One test is infinitely better than zero.

📖 Chapter 9

Avoiding Spam Filters and Staying Compliant

"Trust is the foundation of email marketing. Lose it, and you lose everything."

"Trust is the foundation of email marketing. Lose it, and you lose everything."

The inbox is sacred space. People invited you in, and spam filters stand guard to make sure you behave. If your emails get flagged as spam, you don't just miss sales — you damage your reputation and risk losing your email privileges entirely.

_This chapter will help you stay in good standing — with both subscribers and the law.

📦 *Reflection Box*

Think about your own inbox.

What makes you hit "Spam" immediately?

Overly pushy subject lines?

Endless sales pitches?

Messages that feel like they don't belong to you?

Why Emails Go to Spam

Spam filters look for patterns of abuse. Common red flags include:

Overuse of ALL CAPS or too many exclamation marks!!!

Misleading subject lines

Excessive links or attachments

Low engagement (too many people ignoring or deleting your emails)

Using a free "from" address (like Gmail or Yahoo) instead of a domain email

---

Staying Compliant: The Laws You Need to Know

💡 *Key Insight*

Deliverability isn't just about avoiding spammy words. It's about building trust with subscribers and internet service providers (ISPs).

Depending on where you and your subscribers live, you need to follow certain rules:

- ➢ CAN-SPAM (U.S.) – Requires an unsubscribe link and accurate sender info.
- ➢ CASL (Canada) – Requires express consent before emailing.
- ➢ GDPRDPR (Europe) – Strict on data privacy and consent.

At a minimum, your emails should always include:

- ➢ ☑ Clear permission (they opted in)
- ➢ ☑ A visible unsubscribe link
- ➢ ☑ Your physical mailing address

🌱 *Gentle Reminder*
Compliance isn't about limiting you — it's about protecting relationships.

Best Practices for Staying Out of Spam

Use a custom domain email (you@yourbusiness.com

- ➢ Keep your list clean (remove inactive subscribers).
- ➢ Avoid spam-trigger words like "FREE $$$" or "Act NOW."
- ➢ Encourage replies — real engagement helps deliverability.
- ➢ Don't buy or rent lists (ever).

Don't take it personally. Unsubscribes are natural — and often healthy. Make it easy, and don't try to guilt-trip people.

💡 Key Insight

A smooth unsubscribe experience can actually improve your brand reputation.

Make it easy, and don't try to guilt-trip people.

Write a friendly unsubscribe line for the bottom of your email.
☞ *Example: "No hard feelings. If these emails aren't your thing, you can unsubscribe anytime here."*

☑️ Action Steps for Chapter 9

➢ Review your emails for compliance (unsubscribe link, sender info, physical address).
➢ Switch to a domain email if you're still using Gmail/Yahoo.
➢ Remove inactive subscribers every few months.
➢ Reframe unsubscribes as a healthy part of growth.

🍷 *Gentle Reminder*
The goal isn't to keep everyone — it's to keep the right ones.

📖 Chapter 10

Monetization — Turning Subscribers into Customers

"An email list isn't just a community. It's a business asset."

Building your list is the foundation. Writing engaging emails is the craft. But at some point, your list has to support your business. Monetization is not about squeezing every dollar — it's about serving your subscribers so well that buying from you feels like the natural next step.

📦 *Reflection Box*

Think about the last time you bought something through email.
What made you trust the sender?
Did the offer feel like a natural fit?
Or did it feel pushy and out of place?
The Mindset of Email Sales

Selling through email works best when it feels like a continuation of the relationship, not a break in it.

Principles to remember:

- ➢ Lead with value, then make the offer.
- ➢ Present the product as a solution, not just a pitch.
- ➢ Keep your offers aligned with the reason people joined your list.

💡 Key Insight

The best sales emails don't feel like sales emails. They feel like help arriving at the right time.

Proven Monetization Methods

Direct Product Offers – Promoting your core products or services.

Upsells & Cross-Sells – Offering add-ons or complementary items.

Affiliate Marketing – Promoting trusted partners' products.

Memberships & Subscriptions – Recurring revenue models.

Courses & Digital Products – Scaling your knowledge.

Webinars & Workshops – Selling through education. Upsells & Cross-Sells – Offering add-ons or complementary items.

Affiliate Marketing – Promoting trusted partners' products.

Memberships & Subscriptions – Recurring revenue models.

Courses & Digital Products – Scaling your knowledge.

Webinars & Workshops – Selling through education.

🍷 *Gentle Reminder*
Monetization should never betray trust. If you wouldn't recommend it to your best friend, don't promote it.

Crafting Sales Sequences

A sales sequence is a short, focused automation designed to move someone from interest to purchase.

> A simple 4-email sales sequence:
> Problem – Highlight the pain point.
> Possibility – Paint the vision of a better outcome.
> Proof – Share testimonials, case studies, or your story.
> Pitch – Present your offer clearly with a call-to-action.

📦 Reflection Box

Which product or service in your business feels like the easiest yes for your subscribers? That's where to start your first sales sequence.

Pricing Psychology

Email is a great place to use gentle nudges that help subscribers decide.

Anchoring – Show the "regular" price, then your offer.

Scarcity – Limited spots, limited time (used ethically).

Bonuses – Extra value for quick action.

✏️ Quick Exercise

Write one subject line for each stage of a sales sequence:

👉 Problem: "Struggling to keep up with content?"

👉 Possibility: "Imagine having 30 days of posts done in 1 hour"

👉 Proof: "Here's how Sarah doubled her sales with this system"

👉 Pitch: "Your all-in-one toolkit is waiting for you"

Affiliate Monetization

If you don't have your own products yet, affiliate marketing can be a win-win. Promote tools and products you genuinely use and love, and earn commission when subscribers buy through your link.

💡 Key Insight

The key word in affiliate marketing is trust. One bad recommendation can cost you subscribers.

☑ Action Steps for Chapter 10

> ➤ Choose one monetization method to focus on.
> ➤ Map out a simple 4-email sales sequence.
> ➤ Test a small, aligned offer with your list.
> ➤ Track conversions and refine.

🌱 Gentle Reminder

*Selling through email isn't about pressure. It's about alignment —
the right offer, to the right people, at the right time.*

📖 Chapter 11

Case Studies and Real-World Examples

"Stories teach what strategies can't."

Up to now, we've covered strategies, frameworks, and action steps. But theory becomes powerful when you see how it's been lived out in real businesses. In this chapter, we'll look at real-world examples of entrepreneurs and companies who used email marketing to grow — and what you can learn from them.

🎁 *Reflection Box*
Think about your favourite brand or expert you follow online.
Have you ever joined their email list?
Did they make you feel connected, educated, or sold to?
What stuck with you most about their approach?

Case Study 1: The Solo Coach

Challenge: A health coach struggled to get clients from Instagram alone.

Solution: She created a lead magnet called "7 Quick Morning Habits for More Energy" and built a welcome sequence around it.

Result: Within 3 months, she grew her list to 500 subscribers and booked 12 new coaching clients — simply by showing up weekly with helpful tips and a gentle call-to-action.

💡 Lesson: A simple lead magnet + consistent emails can turn a small list into paying clients.

Case Study 2: The Ecommerce Shop

Challenge: An online boutique had abandoned cart rates over 70%.

Solution: They set up an abandoned cart sequence:

Email 1 (1 hour later): Reminder with product image.

Email 2 (24 hours later): Social proof ("Others are loving this item").

Email 3 (48 hours later): Limited stock reminder.

Result: 18% of abandoned carts were recovered.

💡 Lesson: Automations don't just save time — they save sales.

Case Study 3: The Creator

Challenge: A podcaster wanted to monetize her audience.

Solution: She used ConvertKit to segment her list by topic interests (business, lifestyle, or mindset). Then she created tailored offers: a mini-course, a digital planner, and a membership.

Result: Instead of blasting one generic offer, she matched the right product to the right audience — tripling her revenue in 6 months.

💡 Lesson: Segmentation = higher conversions.

🏆 *Gentle Reminder*
Every big success started with one small test.

Case Study 4: The Nonprofit

Challenge: A nonprofit wanted to increase donations but didn't want to pressure supporters.

Solution: They shared a storytelling-driven nurture sequence: highlighting one person impacted by their mission each week. At the end of the month, they sent a donation appeal framed as "help us share more stories like this."

Result: Their monthly donations doubled, and engagement (opens/replies) skyrocketed.

💡 Lesson: Storytelling builds emotional connection — and connection drives action.

Write a "mini case study" of your own (even if it's just one success).

👉 *What was the problem?* 👉 *What did you try?*

👉 *What happened?* 👉 *What lesson did you learn?*

Sharing these with your own audience builds your authority too.

☑ Action Steps for Chapter 11

➢ Pick one case study model that mirrors your business.
➢ Identify which strategies you can borrow.
➢ Draft your own mini case study to share with your list.
➢ Keep building your "success file" — stories sell.

💡 Key Insight

People learn best from stories. Use them not just to teach, but to inspire and connect.

📖 Conclusion

Your Long-Term Email Strategy

"Email marketing is not a sprint. It's a rhythm."

By now, you've learned how to:

- ➤ Build a high-quality list
- ➤ Create lead magnets that attract the right people
- ➤ Write emails that connect and get opened
- ➤ Set up automations that save time and grow sales
- ➤ Personalize and segment for deeper relevance
- ➤ Test and measure for constant improvement
- ➤ Stay compliant and build trust
- ➤ Monetize with integrity
- ➤ Learn from real-world success stories

But knowledge alone won't change your business. Consistency will.

📦 Reflection Box
Where do you see yourself one year from now if you follow through?
How many subscribers could you realistically grow?
How much more confident would you feel about selling?
What would "success" look like in your inbox?
The Long Game

Email marketing isn't about a single campaign. It's about building a relationship engine that grows with you.

Think in terms of seasons, not sprints:

- Season of Building – Focus on growing your list with the right people.
- Season of Nurturing – Deliver consistent value, stories, and tips.
- Season of Selling – Confidently present aligned offers.
- Season of Refining – Test, tweak, and improve based on data.

💡 Key Insight

Your list is not just names and emails. It's people. Each with their own goals, struggles, and hopes. Treat them like humans, not numbers.

Staying Consistent

- Pick a sending schedule you can actually keep.
- Commit to showing up, even if your list is small.
- Remember that every email is practice — your writing will get better with time.

🏺 Gentle Reminder
The best time to start was yesterday. The second-best time is today.

☑ Final Action Steps

- ➤ Pick one lead magnet, one sequence, and one sending schedule.
- ➤ Stick with it for 90 days.
- ➤ Track your results — numbers tell stories too.
- ➤ Keep refining and keep showing up.

💡 Closing Thought

Your inbox influence grows one message at a time. Write with purpose, lead with heart, and remember: the real power of email is not in technology, but in connection.

Appendix A: Affiliate Email Templates

Why It Matters

Affiliate marketing is one of the easiest ways to monetize your email list — but only if it's done with integrity. Your subscribers trust you. They'll buy from your recommendations if they believe you're sharing something genuinely useful. A well-written affiliate email should feel like advice from a friend, not a sales pitch.

How to Use This Section

> ➢ Pick a product or service you believe in.
> ➢ Choose the template that best matches your audience and offer.
> ➢ Personalize it with your story, benefits, and tone.
> ➢ Add your affiliate link.
> ➢ Test it with a small segment before sending it to your whole list.

Template 1: Personal Recommendation

Subject: [First Name], I think you'll love this…

Hi [First Name],

I've been using [Product/Service] and it's made such a difference in [specific area].

Here's why I love it:

[Benefit 1]

[Benefit 2]

[Benefit 3]

If you'd like to check it out, here's the link: [Affiliate Link].

Warmly,

[Your Name]

✉ Template 2: Story-Based Approach

Subject: How I solved [problem]

Hi [First Name],

Not long ago, I struggled with [challenge]. It was stressful, and I wasn't sure what to try next.

Then I found [Product/Service], and here's what happened:

[Share short transformation story].

If you're in the same place, you might find this helpful too: [Affiliate Link].

With care,

[Your Name]

📧 Template 3: Urgency & Value

Subject: Only available until [date]

Hi [First Name],

 Just a quick note — [Product/Service] is offering [bonus/discount] until [date].

 If this is something you've been considering, now's the best time to jump in.

 Here's the link: [Affiliate Link].

 I wouldn't share this if I didn't believe it could help you.

All the best,

[Your Name]

📝 Notes & Customization Space

Affiliate Product I Want to Promote:

_____

Why I Believe in It:

_____

My Audience's Pain Point:

_____

How This Product Solves It:

_____

Affiliate Link:

_____

📑 Appendix B: Lead Magnet Creation Worksheet

Why It Matters

Your lead magnet is the very first impression most subscribers will have of you. Done well, it answers a burning question or solves a small problem for free — creating trust, excitement, and a natural step toward your paid offers.

A strong lead magnet should be:

➤ Specific – solves one clear problem.
➤ Actionable – helps your subscriber take a quick win.
➤ Relevant – directly linked to your paid offer.
➤ Easy to consume – no one wants a 200-page eBook as their first taste.

Common Lead Magnet Formats

➤ Checklist (simple, fast win)
➤ Guide or Mini eBook (in-depth but focused)
➤ Video Tutorial or Mini-Course
➤ Quiz or Assessment
➤ Template or Script Pack
➤ Resource List (tools, apps, books)

✏️ Brainstorm Your Lead Magnet

> ⚠ Avoid: Generic "newsletters," vague "updates," or freebies that don't connect to your actual business.

1. Who is this for?

(Describe your ideal subscriber.)

2. What problem does it solve quickly?

(Keep it small and specific, like "5-minute makeup routine for busy moms" instead of "Makeup tips.")

3. What format will you use?

- ☐ Checklist
- ☐ Guide
- ☐ Video Tutorial
- ☐ Quiz
- ☐ Template
- ☐ Resource List

Other:

_____

4. Title Ideas

(Scribble at least 3 — clarity beats cleverness!)

5. Next Step for the Subscriber

(What will they be ready to do after consuming your lead magnet?)

Example

If you sell wellness products, a good lead magnet could be:

"7-Day Energy Reset Checklist" (fast win, ties into supplements)

"The Busy Person's Guide to Better Sleep" (solves a pain point, connects to lifestyle products)

📝 Notes

Lead Magnet I'm Creating:

_____

_____

Delivery Method (PDF, video, etc.):

_____

_____

Where I'll Promote It:

_____

_____

📑 Appendix C: Platform Comparison Checklist

Why It Matters

Your email marketing platform is the backbone of your inbox influence. The wrong tool can frustrate you, waste money, or limit your growth — but the right one feels like a partner in your business.

Instead of chasing shiny new tools, focus on what matters most to your business.

Key Features to Consider

- ☐ Ease of Use – Is the dashboard intuitive, or will you need a manual every time?
- ☐ Automation – Can it create welcome sequences, promo campaigns, and re-engagement flows?
- ☐ Segmentation – Can you tag, group, and personalize easily?
- ☐ Integrations – Does it connect with the tools you already use (e.g., website, social, payments)?
- ☐ Deliverability – Does it have a reputation for getting emails into inboxes (not spam)?
- ☐ Scalability – Will it grow affordably as your list grows?
- ☐ Customer Support – When something breaks, will they help quickly?
- ☐ Cost – Does it fit your budget today and in the future?

Popular Platforms to Explore

- ➤ Mailchimp – Beginner-friendly, good for small lists, limited automation.
- ➤ ConvertKit – Creator-focused, simple automation, great for content-driven businesses.
- ➤ ActiveCampaign – Advanced automation + CRM features, best for scaling.
- ➤ MailerLite – Affordable, clean interface, solid for starters.
- ➤ Klaviyo – Powerful for eCommerce stores, deep integrations with Shopify/online shops.

My Comparison Table

Platform	Ease of Use (1–5)	Automation (1–5)	Segmentation (1–5)	Cost ($/mo)	Notes
Mailchimp					
ConvertKit					
ActiveCampaign					
MailerLite					
Klaviyo					
Decision Prompts					

Which platform matches my current stage?

_____

Which platform will still serve me in 2 years?

_____

Which platform feels easiest for me to actually use consistently?

_____

📄 Final Choice

Chosen Platform:

_____

Reason I Picked It:

_____

📑 Appendix D: Automation Sequence Builder

Why It Matters

Email automation saves you hours and builds trust by ensuring the right message reaches the right person at the right time. Instead of writing each email manually, you create a sequence once — and it works in the background, nurturing subscribers, answering questions, and leading them toward the next step.

Think of automation as your digital assistant: reliable, consistent, and always on.

Types of Sequences You'll Need

1. Welcome Sequence (New Subscribers)

Goal: Build trust + deliver lead magnet.

> ➤ Email 1: Deliver freebie + introduce yourself
> ➤ Email 2: Share your story (why you do what you do)
> ➤ Email 3: Provide quick win tip or resource
> ➤ Email 4: Invite to join your community / product trial

2. Nurture Sequence (Warm Relationship)

Goal: Share value + deepen connection.

> ➤ Weekly or bi-weekly tips
> ➤ Personal stories or lessons
> ➤ Gentle nudges toward products/services

3. Promo Sequence (Sales Campaigns)

Goal: Convert subscribers into buyers.

- ➢ Email 1: Introduce offer
- ➢ Email 2: Show benefits + testimonials
- ➢ Email 3: Urgency reminder / "cart closing"

4. Re-Engagement Sequence (Inactive Subscribers)

Goal: Wake up dormant subscribers.

- ➢ Email 1: "Still want to hear from me?"
- ➢ Email 2: "Here's what you missed" + highlight top content
- ➢ Email 3: Final reminder before removing them

🖋 Build Your Own Sequence

Step 1: Choose the goal of your sequence

- ☐ Welcome
- ☐ Nurture
- ☐ Promo
- ☐ Re-Engagement
- ☐ Other:

_____

_____

Step 2: Decide how many emails you'll send

- ☐ 3
- ☐ 5
- ☐ 7+

Step 3: Map the flow

Email #	Subject Line Idea	Purpose (story, tip, offer)	CTA (action you want them to take)
1 _____			
2 _____			
3 _____			
4 _____			
5 _____			

Example: Welcome Sequence

Email #	Subject	Purpose	CTA

1. "Here's your free guide!" - Deliver lead magnet + thank them - Download guide

2. "A little about me..." - Share your story - Follow on social / reply

3. "Quick win for you today" - Give actionable tip - Try resource

4. "Want more support?" - Introduce offer or community - Join program

📝 Notes

My Sequence Goal:

_____

Next Steps to Set It Up:

_____

Automation Platform I'll Use:

_____

Appendix E: Segmentation Planner

Why It Matters

Not all subscribers are the same — so why send them all the same emails? Segmentation is how you make your emails feel personal, relevant, and timely. Done right, it boosts open rates, click-throughs, and sales because your subscribers feel like you're speaking directly to them.

Think of it as moving from broadcasting to conversing.

Common Segments to Consider

- New Subscribers – Just joined, eager to hear from you.
- Engaged Readers – They open/click regularly.
- Buyers – People who have purchased at least once.
- Repeat Buyers / VIPs – Your loyal fans.
- Inactive Subscribers – Haven't opened in 60–90 days.
- Interests-Based – Tagged by lead magnet topic, webinar signup, or quiz result.

📐 Plan Your Segments

Step 1: Define Key Groups in Your Business

(Think: Where does your business model need tailored messages?)

Step 2: Match Segments to Goals

Segment	Goal	Type of Emails They Need
New Subscribers	Build trust	deliver freebie
Welcome sequence	Engaged Readers	Deepen relationship
Tips, value content	Buyers Increase product use	Education, upsell
VIPs	Reward loyalty	Exclusive offers
Inactive Subs	Wake them up or remove	Re-engagement
Interests-Based	Match content to topic	Niche tips, offers

Example Flow

➢ Subscriber downloads "Healthy Snack Guide" → tagged as Nutrition Interest.

- ➢ Subscriber attends Sleep Webinar → tagged as Sleep Interest.
- ➢ Subscriber buys Protein Shake Pack → tagged as Customer: Product X.
- ➢ Now, instead of sending all three the same promo, you can:
- ➢ Send Nutrition Interest people a recipe email.
- ➢ Send Sleep Interest people a bedtime tips email.
- ➢ Send Customers an upsell on complementary products.

✎ My Segmentation Map

Core Segment:

_____

Emails to Send:

_____

Core Segment:

_____

Emails to Send:

_____

Core Segment:

_____

Emails to Send:

_____

📑 **Notes**

Tags I Will Use:

_____

Automation Rules I Need:

_____

Next Steps:

_____

_____

Appendix F: Smart Tagging Cheat Sheet

Why It Matters

Tags are like sticky notes you attach to your subscribers. They track behavior, preferences, and interactions so you can send the right email at the right time. Without tags, everyone looks the same — with tags, you can see exactly who downloaded what, bought what, or engaged when.

Smart tagging turns your email list from a crowd into individuals you understand.

Common Tagging Categories

> By Source
> Downloaded Lead Magnet: [Name of Lead Magnet]
> Signed up via [Landing Page/Event]
> Referred by [Affiliate/Partner]
> By Behavior
> Clicked on [Link/Product]
> Attended Webinar: [Date/Topic]
> Watched Training Video: [Title]
> By Purchase
> Purchased: [Product Name]
> Upsell Purchased: [Product Name]
> VIP Customer (spent over $___)
> By Engagement
> Opens 50%+ emails → Highly Engaged
> No opens in 60 days → Inactive
> Clicked on survey link → Interested in X

Smart Tagging Rules

Rule 1: Tag Actions, Not Just People

E.g., instead of "Subscriber A = Health Enthusiast," tag them as:

- ➤ Downloaded "Healthy Recipes PDF"
- ➤ Clicked "Protein Shake" link
- ➤ Purchased "Wellness Starter Pack"

Rule 2: Keep Tags Simple & Consistent

Examples:

- ➤ "LeadMagnet_HealthySnacks"
- ➤ "Purchase_ProteinShake"
- ➤ "Webinar_Sleep_2025"

Rule 3: Use Tags to Trigger Automation

E.g., "If tagged: Webinar_Sleep → Start Sleep Nurture Sequence."

My Tagging Plan

Lead Magnet Tags I'll Use:

_____

Purchase Tags I'll Use:

_____

Engagement Tags I'll Use:

_____

Automation Triggers to Build:

_____

📝 **Notes** Keep a Tagging Glossary (like a master list) so you and your team don't get lost. Over-tagging = chaos. Smart, Consistent tagging = clarity and power.

Appendix G: A/B Testing Tracker

Why It Matters

Guessing what your audience wants rarely works. A/B testing (also called split testing) lets you compare two versions of an email to see which performs better. Over time, small improvements add up to big gains in opens, clicks, and conversions.

Think of it as being a scientist in your own inbox — experiment, measure, learn, improve.

What You Can Test

Subject Line Tests

- ➢ Short vs. long subject line
- ➢ Question vs. statement
- ➢ Curiosity-driven vs. direct offer
- ➢ Content Tests
- ➢ Plain text style vs. image-heavy
- ➢ Long story vs. short punchy message
- ➢ Single call-to-action vs. multiple links

Timing Tests

- ➢ Morning vs. evening
- ➢ Weekday vs. weekend

Offer Tests

- ➢ Bonus A vs. Bonus B
- ➢ Discount % vs. Free Shipping

✎ Testing Guidelines

Test one variable at a time. If you change both subject line and timing, you won't know what worked.

Use a big enough sample size. At least 100–200 subscribers per version for reliable results.

Run the test for at least 24–48 hours before declaring a winner.

Always record results. What you learn today saves you time in the future.

📑 A/B Testing Log

Test Date: _____

Type of Test: _____

Version A: _____

Version B: _____

Open Rate A: _____

Open Rate B: _____

Click Rate A: _____

Click Rate B: _____

Winner: _____

Notes:

_____

_____

_____

_____

_____

Example Test

- ➢ Test Date: March 12
- ➢ Type: Subject Line
- ➢ Version A: "5 Quick Energy Hacks"
- ➢ Version B: "Boost Your Energy in 5 Minutes"
- ➢ Result: A = 22% open rate, B = 31% open rate
- ➢ Winner: Version B
- ➢ Lesson: Specific benefit + time frame = stronger curiosity

Reflection Questions

What types of tests do I want to run first?

_____

How often will I run A/B tests? (e.g., 1x per month)

_____

What's the most surprising result I've seen so far?

_____

📑 Appendix H: Deliverability Checklist

Why It Matters

You can write the most brilliant email in the world, but if it lands in the spam folder, it's invisible. Deliverability is the art and science of making sure your messages reach the inbox. Think of it as building a good reputation with the "gatekeepers" (Gmail, Outlook, Yahoo).

Strong deliverability = more opens, more clicks, more sales.

✅ Deliverability Best Practices

1. Build a Clean List

- ☐ Only email people who opted in
- ☐ Remove hard bounces (invalid emails)
- ☐ Re-engage or remove inactive subscribers regularly

2. Authenticate Your Domain

- ☐ Set up SPF
- ☐ Set up DKIM
- ☐ Set up DMARC

(Your email platform usually provides step-by-step guides — once set, you rarely touch these again.)

3. Write Spam-Safe Content

- ☐ Avoid spam trigger words: "FREE!!!," "Click NOW," "$$$$"
- ☐ Use balanced text-to-image ratio (don't send image-only emails)
- ☐ Use natural, conversational tone

4. Be Recognizable

- ☐ Use a consistent "From Name" (preferably you or your brand) Don't switch sending addresses often
- ☐ Use a professional domain email (yourname@yourbusiness.com), not Gmail/Hotmail

5. Test Before Sending

- ☐ Send to yourself (Gmail, Outlook, Yahoo if possible)
- ☐ Use your platform's spam score checker (if available)
- ☐ Preview on mobile and desktop

6. Respect Engagement

- ☐ Don't send too often (burnout risk)
- ☐ Don't send too little (cold list risk)
- ☐ Ask readers to reply — replies improve deliverability!

📝 Deliverability Maintenance Log

Date:

_____

Action Taken (clean list, re-engagement, SPF/DKIM check, etc.):

_____

Notes:

_____
_____
_____
_____
_____

Quick Pro Tip

💡 Even big-name marketers get caught in spam sometimes. The difference is: they test, adjust, and keep refining. Think of deliverability as a fitness routine for your email list — it only works if you keep at it.

Appendix I: Compliance Setup Guide

Why It Matters

Email marketing is powerful, but it also comes with rules. Laws like CAN-SPAM (USA), GDPR (Europe), and CASL (Canada) are designed to protect consumers from spam and shady practices.

Following compliance isn't just about avoiding fines — it's about building trust and credibility. When subscribers know you respect their privacy, they're more likely to stick around (and buy from you).

Compliance Checklist

1. Permission First

- ☐ Only email people who opted in (no purchased lists).
- ☐ Use clear, plain language on sign-up forms ("Get weekly tips," not "You may receive marketing messages...").

2. Identification

- ☐ Use your real name or business name in the "From" field.
- ☐ Provide a valid physical mailing address at the bottom of every email.

3. Easy Unsubscribe

- ☐ Include a visible unsubscribe link in every email.
- ☐ Process unsubscribe requests immediately (no hoops)

4. Honest Subject Lines

- ☐ Don't mislead ("Re: your invoice" when it's really a promo = 🚫).
- ☐ Subject lines must match the content of the email.

5. Record Keeping

- ☐ Store proof of opt-in (many platforms track this automatically).
- ☐ Document consent dates and methods.

🌐 Quick Guide to Major Laws

CAN-SPAM (USA)

- ➤ Clear opt-out option.
- ➤ Honest subject lines.
- ➤ Include physical address.

GDPR (Europe)

- ➤ Explicit consent (no pre-checked boxes).
- ➤ Right to access, edit, or delete personal data.
- ➤ Extra care when handling sensitive data.

CASL (Canada)

- ➤ Express consent required (implied consent expires after 2 years).
- ➤ Unsubscribe must be quick and easy.
- ➤ Fines can be steep for violations.

✏️ Compliance Self-Check

Do I have proof of consent for every person on my list? _____

Does every email I send include my business address? _____

Do my subject lines always reflect what's inside? _____

Can someone unsubscribe in one click? _____

📝 Notes

Next Action I Need to Take:

_____

_____

Compliance Gaps I've Noticed:

_____

_____

How I'll Fix Them:

_____

_____

📑 Appendix J: Promo Email Sequence Template Pack

Why It Matters

When it's time to promote an offer, many entrepreneurs freeze. "What do I say? How often should I send?" A proven promo sequence takes away the guesswork and lets you sell with confidence — without sounding pushy.

The key is to layer trust + value + urgency over several emails instead of cramming everything into one.

☑️ 3-Email Promo Sequence

Email 1: Introduce the Offer

- ➤ **Subject:** "Something new for you..."
- ➤ **Goal:** Introduce the product/service and connect it to a problem your audience cares about.

Structure:

- ➤ Acknowledge the pain point.
- ➤ Introduce your solution.
- ➤ Share 1–2 benefits.
- ➤ Link to more info or sales page.

Email 2: Story + Proof

- ➤ **Subject:** "How [Name/Customer] solved [problem]"
- ➤ **Goal:** Build trust with a testimonial, case study, or your own story.

Structure:

- ➢ Share transformation story.
- ➢ Highlight specific results.
- ➢ Tie back to benefits.
- ➢ Include call-to-action (CTA).

Email 3: Urgency Reminder

- ➢ **Subject:** "Last chance to grab this"
- ➢ **Goal:** Create urgency with a deadline or limited spots.

Structure:

- ➢ Restate the offer.
- ➢ Repeat benefits.
- ➢ Add urgency ("Offer ends tonight").
- ➢ CTA link.

☑ 5-Email Extended Promo Sequence

Email 1: Teaser/Announcement

- ➢ Build curiosity before launch.

Email 2: Full Offer Reveal

- ➢ Share all the details, benefits, and value.

Email 3: Story + Social Proof

- ➢ Case studies, testimonials, screenshots.

Email 4: Overcome Objections

- ➢ Tackle common hesitations (time, money, results).

Email 5: Final Reminder

- ➢ Urgency push before doors close.

✅ Seasonal/Bonus Promo Ideas

- ➢ "New Year Reset" (fresh starts)
- ➢ "Summer Special" (limited-time bundle)
- ➢ "Holiday Gift Guide" (curated picks)
- ➢ "Birthday/Anniversary" (personal touch)

🔨 Promo Sequence Builder

Email #	Subject Line Idea	Main Message	CTA
1			
2			
3			
4			
5			

📝 Notes

My Next Promo Offer:

_____

Launch Dates:

_____

Incentives (bonuses/discounts):

_____

Main Objections to Overcome:

_____

Appendix K: Case Study Swipe File

Why It Matters

Stories sell. Numbers prove. Together, they build trust. Case studies give you evidence that email marketing works — and they also give you patterns you can swipe and apply to your own business.

Think of this swipe file as a library of inspiration: when you're not sure how to frame your own results, borrow the structure here.

Case Study Format (Swipe Template)

- ➤ The Challenge – What problem did the business face?
- ➤ The Strategy – What approach or email tactic did they try?
- ➤ The Results – What happened (numbers + story)?
- ➤ The Lesson – What can you take away?

Example Case Studies

Case Study 1:

- ➤ Boosting Engagement with Personalization
- ➤ Challenge: A wellness coach had a 25% open rate but very low clicks.
- ➤ Strategy: Segmented list into "Nutrition Interest" and "Fitness Interest." Sent tailored weekly tips.
- ➤ Results: Click-through rates doubled from 3% → 6%. Engagement increased overall.
- ➤ Lesson: Even small personalization (like interests) can dramatically improve results.

Case Study 2: Re-Engagement Campaign

- ➤ Challenge: An online boutique had 2,000 inactive subscribers (no opens for 90+ days).
- ➤ Strategy: Sent a 3-email re-engagement sequence with subject lines like "Do you still want to hear from us?"
- ➤ Results: 400 people re-engaged, 1,600 were removed (cleaning the list improved deliverability).
- ➤ Lesson: Don't be afraid to prune your list — a smaller, active list is more profitable than a large, dead one.

- ➤ Case Study 3: Launching with a Welcome Sequence
- ➤ Challenge: A course creator had a new online program but no promo plan.
- ➤ Strategy: Built a 4-part welcome sequence with value tips leading into a course invitation.
- ➤ Results: 150 sales in the first two weeks.
- ➤ Lesson: A strong welcome sequence can double as your first promo campaign.

📝 My Case Study Notes

Business/Offer:

_____
_____

Challenge:

_____
_____

Strategy Used:

_____
_____

Results:

_____

_____

—

Lesson Learned:

_____

_____

📝 Quick Pro Tip

💡 Keep your own mini "case study log." Anytime you run a campaign, record the challenge, strategy, results, and lesson. Over time, you'll build your own swipe file tailored to your audience.

🌱 *Gentle Reminder*
The goal isn't to keep everyone — it's to keep the right ones.

Appendix L: 90-Day Action Plan Printable

Why It Matters

Knowledge without action = no results. This 90-day planner helps you implement email marketing step by step, so you don't feel overwhelmed. Break it down, stay consistent, and watch your influence grow.

Think of this as your roadmap for the next 3 months.

How to Use This Planner

➢ Pick 1 focus per month (list building, automation, monetization, etc.).
➢ Break it into weekly action steps.
➢ Review progress every week and adjust as needed.

Month 1: Foundation

Goal:

_____

_____

Weekly Actions:

_____

_____

Week 1:

_____

_____

Week 2:

_____

_____

Week 3:

_____

_____

Week 4:

_____

_____

🔼 Month 2: Growth

Goal:

_____

_____

Weekly Actions:

Week 5:

_____

_____

Week 6:

_____

_____

Week 7:

_____

_____

Week 8:

_____

_____

🔺 Month 3: Monetization

Goal:

_____

_____

Weekly Actions:

Week 9:

_____

_____

Week 10:

_____

_____

Week 11:

_____

_____

Week 12:

_____

_____

Progress Tracker

Week Action Completed? (✓)	Notes / Wins Next Steps
1	
2	
3	
4	
5	
6	
7	
8	
9	
10	
11	
12	

Reflection Prompts

My biggest win this quarter was:

_____

_____

What didn't go as planned:

_____

_____

One thing I'll do differently next time:

_____

_____

Appendix M: Next Steps Worksheet

Why It Matters

Finishing this book is only the beginning. The magic happens when you take consistent, heart-centered action. This worksheet helps you capture your key insights, commit to your next steps, and stay focused on building long-term success.

Step 1: Capture Your Wins

- ➢ The 3 biggest "aha" moments I had in this book:
- ➢ The strategies I'm most excited to try:

Step 2: Define Your Next Focus

- ➢ In the next 30 days, I will:
- ➢ In the next 90 days, my email marketing will look like this:

Step 3: Tools & Resources I Need

- ☐ Platform I'll use: _____
- ☐ Lead magnet idea: _____
- ☐ Automation I'll set up first: _____
- ☐ Segment/Tag strategy: _____
- ☐ Compliance steps to review: _____

✎ Step 4: My Accountability Plan

Who will I share my goals with?

_____

_____

_____

How often will I review my progress?

_____

_____

_____

What reward will I give myself when I hit my next milestone?

_____

_____

_____

✨ Closing Words

If you've made it this far, I want to say a heartfelt thank you.

You've invested your time, your attention, and your energy into learning how to grow your influence through the inbox. That tells me one thing: you care deeply about the people you serve.

Email marketing isn't just about technology, subject lines, or open rates. It's about people. It's about showing up consistently, with value and authenticity, in a space where trust matters most.

As you put these strategies into practice, remember:

⛰ Progress matters more than perfection.

⛰ Small, steady steps will compound over time.

⛰ Your words have the power to influence, inspire, and create real change.

So go ahead — press send. Share your voice. Build your community. And trust that the right people will be glad you showed up.

With gratitude and encouragement,

Debbie Blower